Contents

Mitre

Introduction

Rugby has been played in a form which would be recognisable to modern teams for over one hundred and fifty years. The rules have been gradually modified, sometimes in the interests of safety, but it remains a hard, fast and exciting game. It calls for both individual skills and team skills, and there is plenty of physical contact.

Rugby is a game where a player can shine as an individual, but must also work within the framework of a team. It demands communication, co-operation, reliability and the need to mix with others. Rugby develops you not only as a player but also as a person; friendships started on the rugby field often last a lifetime.

Although it is still primarily a men's game, women's rugby is a fast-growing area of the sport. The movement to women's teams started in universities and polytechnics, and has rapidly spread to many other rugby clubs.

So take up rugby union, and play it to the highest standard you can. You may be taking the first steps on a career which could lead to you playing in the great stadia of the rugby world and giving immense pleasure to thousands of supporters!

Women's rugby – a fast-growing part of the sport

1 What the game is all about

Rugby is a game played by two small armies, called teams, each of which is determined to score points by carrying a ball over the opponents' goal line and touching it on the ground, or by kicking it over the cross-bar of their goalposts. Naturally, the team with the ball is the one which will score, so the game really becomes one long battle for possession. The players in the teams are divided broadly into those whose main job is to gain possession of the ball – the *forwards* – and those who are expected to score with it – the *backs*.

Possession is gained by simply seizing the ball during open play, or as a result of successful strategy during one of the formal "set pieces", such as a *line-out* or a *scrum*.

Once your side has possession, the object is to get the ball over your opponent's goal line. This can rarely be done in one attempt, so much of the team effort goes into *making ground*. Every yard gained is one yard less that your team will have to carry the ball through the opposition, so you must never miss an opportunity to make ground.

Unlike soccer, in rugby the players are allowed to handle the ball, run with it, and tackle an opponent who is in possession of it by grabbing hold of him and wrestling him to the ground. As the ball is oval, its bounce is almost impossible to predict, so dribbling and passing on the ground are not always effective: the essence of rugby is the running pass hand-to-hand.

In the rules for passing, we meet another peculiarity which makes rugby special: *you are not allowed to pass forwards*. This is the rule which causes magnificent sweeping movements when a line of fast-running backs charge down the field in echelon, passing the ball from one to another while somehow managing to find the gaps in the opposition.

A determined battle for possession: Yorkshire's John Liley is well tackled in a match for under-21s at Twickenham

The scrums, and their close relations, the rucks and the mauls, are struggles for possession which call for strength and technique from everyone involved. Match analysis has shown that as much as half the playing time in a rugby match can be taken up with scrum activity, so a successful team will be fit and well-practised in the scrum.

That sums up a game which is played with great enthusiasm throughout the world, from the muddy winter fields of Britain to the sandy, palm-surrounded pitches of Fiji. Let's take a closer look at the terms used in the game, and at the rules and regulations. Note that when we use the term *rugby* in this book, we are always referring to the union game, and not to the similar game of *rugby league*.

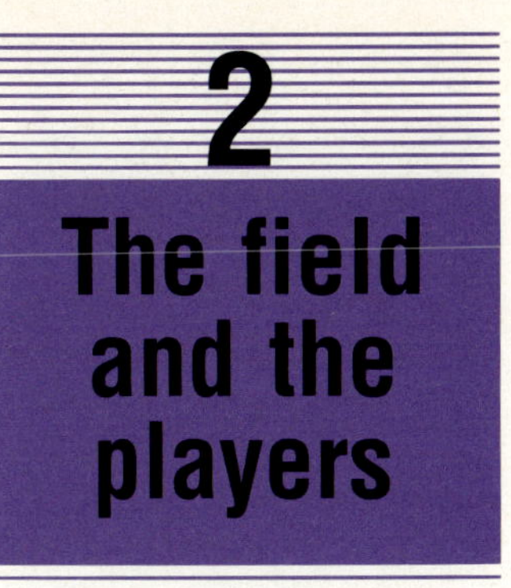

2 The field and the players

The field

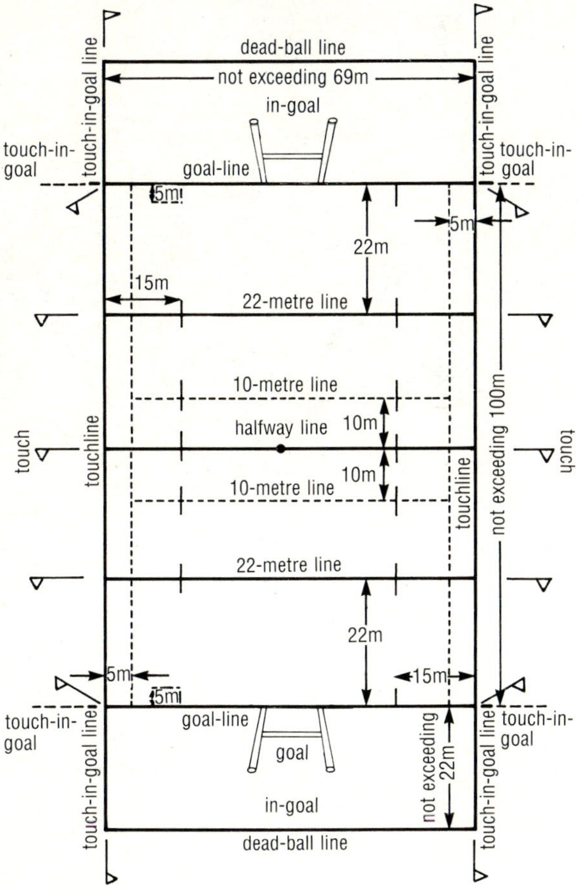

Figure 1 The field

Take up
Rugby Union

The players

Each team has fifteen players. The teams usually wear numbered shirts which indicate the positions in which they play. Although they are grouped into *forwards* and *backs*, any player can score, and there is plenty of scope for individual initiative as well as good solid teamwork. This list shows the names of the positions and the shirt-numbers that the players will usually carry:

1 *Loose head prop* The forward on the left of the front row in the scrum.

2 *Hooker* Middle player in the front row: *hooks* the ball back with his foot.

3 *Tight head prop* The forward on the right of the front row in the scrum.

The *prop forwards* (1 and 3) are often the heftiest players in the team, and have to support the hooker.

Wakefield prop Clive Yemm putting his weight into a try-scoring run

4 and **5** *Lock forwards*, or just *locks*. They are the second row of the scrum. The locks often have the job of jumping for the ball so they are
The locks a

6 and **7** *Flank*
together, bu
quickly as s

8 Simply, *num* ... control at the back of th

All the players from 1 to 8 are forwards, and are usually referred to as *the pack*.

9 *Scrum-half* The player who forms part of the vital link between the backs and the forwards. He puts the ball into the tunnel formed in the scrum, and will usually be the one who passes it to the line of backs when it emerges from scrums, line-outs, rucks and mauls.

10 *Outside-half*, or *fly-half*. The next link in the chain of backs.

11 and **14** *Wingers* Chosen for speed and elusiveness, they should have the ability to score tries by fast runs down the touchline.

12 and **13** *Centre backs*, or just *centres*.

15 *Full back* The last line of defence, but also very important in attack.

The names for numbers 9 to 15 have become shortened over the years: the "half" in *scrum-half* and *fly-half* indicates that these are "half-back" positions, while to be fully correct the *centres* and *wingers* should be "three-quarter backs".

Figure 2 This plan represents the fifteen players in an idealised formation

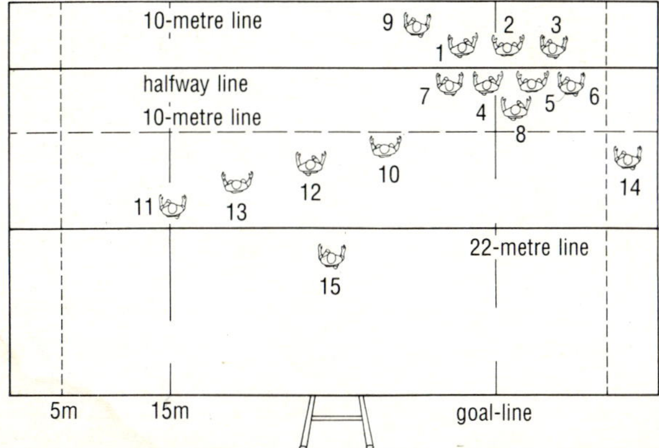

ISBN 0 947655 67 0

First published 1989 by
Springfield Books Limited
Springfield House, Norman Road, Denby Dale, Huddersfield HD8 8TH

Edited, designed and produced by
White Line Press
60 Bradford Road, Stanningley, Leeds LS28 6EF

Editors: Noel Whittall and Philip Gardner
Design: Krystyna Hewitt
Diagrams: Steve Beaumont, IT Design Associates

Printed and bound in Great Britain

Photographic credits
Cover photograph: Associated Sports Photography
Gordon Bunney: pages 6, 9, 11, 13, 16, 18, 19, 23, 26, 29, 33, 34, 35, 38, 42, 44, 47, 58, 60
John Shepherd: page 52
Noel Whittall: pages 15, 25, 28, 31, 55

Take up Rugby Union

Principal contributor:

John Shepherd

Coach to the Yorkshire XV
and Northern Division Under-21 XV

SPRINGFIELD BOOKS LIMITED

SBL

Scrum halves at work. The opposing scrum half is just too slow to stop this safe pass away from the scrum.

One of the players in each team will also be the *captain*. He will normally be a senior member of the side, whose job is to make sure that the team works together for maximum effect.

Reserves and substitutes

In club rugby at senior level, two replacement players are allowed to be available for play in case of injury to team members. They can only be used in this way, and not just as tactical replacements as in some other games. The injured players should only be replaced with the approval of a medically trained person. Before the match starts, it is up to the home side to inform the referee if such a person is available; if not, the referee has to give the approval.

In certain major championships and in international matches, up to six extra players may be available as replacements. At the time of writing, only two may actually be used, but it is very likely that this will be increased to three in due course.

In school rugby, and any game where all the players are under 19, up to six players may be replaced.

Although any player can score, it is usual to look at the team as consisting of three distinct groups:

Front five:	*ball winners*	Numbers 1 to 5
Middle five:	*link, or pivot players*	Numbers 6 to 10
Back five:	*penetrators*	Numbers 11 to 15

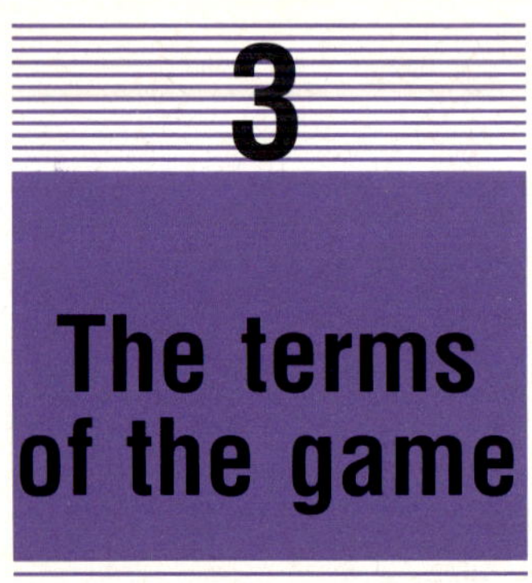

3 The terms of the game

It will be easier to understand the descriptions of play if you meet some of the special terms used in rugby at this early stage. They are deliberately covered very briefly here: fuller explanations will be given at appropriate points throughout the book.

Advantage rule There are many rules concerning play. If they were all applied according to the letter of the law, the referee's whistle would almost always be blowing, and the game would never develop properly. If the infringement of the rule gives an advantage to the non-offending team, the referee will normally allow play to continue.

Conversion When a *try* has been scored, the successful team is allowed to attempt to convert it into a *goal* by kicking the ball over the cross-bar from any point on the field which is directly in front of the place where the try was made. A try which is converted in this way scores six points.

Dead ball The ball is *dead* when it, or the player carrying it, touches or goes over the *touchlines* marking the sides of the field, or the dead-ball lines at the ends of it. It is also dead as soon as the referee stops play for any reason.

Drop-kick The ball is dropped from the player's hands and kicked at the moment of rebound from the ground.

Fair catch Any player who makes a "fair catch" can claim a free-kick. However, this is not as easy as it sounds! You must be inside your own 22-metre line, with both your feet on the ground, and catch the ball directly from a kick or forward throw by an opponent. You should shout "mark" as you make the catch. Fair catches are surprisingly rare in rugby nowadays. Many years ago they were permitted at any place on the field, and "making a mark" was a more common feature of the game.

An easy conversion from the front of the goal. The opposing team are not allowed to move until the kicker has started to run.

Free-kick A free-kick is awarded to the player making a *fair catch*, or to a member of the non-offending team after certain breaches of the rules. A goal cannot be scored directly from a free-kick.

Gain line The *gain line* is an imaginary line drawn across the field at the point where play stops. It follows that it will therefore pass through the centre of the scrum, line-out, ruck or maul which forms at that point. Naturally, the teams are always striving to play beyond the gain line.

A maul forming around the player in possession

Goal As well as by *converting* a *try*, a goal can be scored by kicking the ball over the cross-bar of the opposing goalposts during play or when a *penalty* has been awarded. A *drop-kick* or *place-kick* must be used. The score for a kicked goal is three points.

Grounding The ball is *grounded* when a player presses down onto it with his hands, arms or the upper part of his body.

In-goal The areas at each end of the field of play between the goal lines and the dead-ball lines.

Kick-off The game is started with a *kick-off* in the form of a place-kick from the centre of the halfway line, and re-started in the same way after a goal has been scored and at half-time. Strangely, if a *try* has been made, but not successfully *converted* into a goal, the game re-starts with a *drop*-kick from the halfway line.

Knock-on This is the act of propelling the ball *forwards*, towards the opposing goal-line, with your hands or arms. It is an offence: if the referee thinks the knock-on was deliberate, he will award a penalty kick to the other side. An accidental knock-on results in a scrum.

Line-out A *line-out* is the means of putting the ball back into play after it has been knocked or kicked so that it contacts, or passes over, the *touchlines* which mark the sides of the field. Several members of each team form into parallel rows, and the ball is thrown in between them by a player from the team which did not last touch the ball.

Maul (see also *ruck* and *scrum*) An informal scrum formed around a player who has the ball in his hands.

Offside There are several ways for a player to become offside in rugby. In open play, the general rule is that players who are ahead of a team member who is in possession of the ball are offside, and must not attempt to take *any* part in the game. Indeed, you sometimes have to clear off and keep a 10-metre gap between yourself and an opponent.

It will take some time before you get used to all the offside situations, but it will help if you try to keep these basics in mind:

- You will inevitably get offside at some stage in every game – everyone does, and there is no crime in that. If you don't attempt to take part in the play, you won't be penalised.
- You are only offside when your team has possession, or when you are in front of the last person in your team to play it. If the other side has the ball, you can't be offside.
- If you are offside and one of your players kicks the ball ahead and you find yourself within 10 metres of an opponent waiting for it, you have to clear off fast until the 10-metre gap exists.

The rules regarding offside in scrums and line-outs are dealt with in other sections of this book.

Pack All the forwards forming a *scrum*.

Penalty kick The referee can award a penalty kick to the non-offending side after a breach of the rules such as a foul tackle or an *offside* offence. Attempts at goal with a place-kick (or drop-kick) are allowed from a penalty. All penalty kicks (including the *tap-penalty* – see below) have to pass through the *penalty mark*, which is the point where the penalty was given.

Place-kick The ball is *placed* on the ground before being kicked. This is the usual choice of kick when *converting* a *try*.

Punt This is similar to a *drop-kick*, except that the ball is kicked *before* it bounces on the ground. It is not permitted for an attempt at goal.

Ruck A *ruck* is an informal *scrum*, formed when one or more players from each side gather around the ball when it is on the ground.

Scrum Originally called a *scrummage*, the *scrum* is a method used to re-start the game after play has been stopped because a rule has been broken. The scrum is formed by at least five players from each side binding together with their arms, in rows, and pushing against the other team with their shoulders. A "tunnel" is formed between the legs of the two front rows, into which the ball is put. The action of forming a scrum and working the ball through it is called *scrummaging*.

Tackle A *tackle* is the act of grabbing the player with the ball so that he is brought to the ground. Dangerous ways of tackling are forbidden; these include tripping, tackling a player without the ball, late tackles, tackling high around the head and neck, and tackling by the shirt collar.

A good tackle – just! Even in an attempt at a smother like this, you have to be careful not to take your opponent dangerously by the neck.

Tap-penalty A *penalty kick* in which the ball is tapped with the foot, then picked up and passed.

Touch The ball goes "*into touch*" when it contacts or passes over the *touchline* at the side of the field, or when a player carrying it touches or steps over the line. As the game is re-started at the point where the ball crosses the line, this can be a valuable way for a team to "gain ground". However, special rules apply, as you will see on page 31.

Try A *try* is scored when a player correctly *grounds* the ball on or behind the opposing team's goal line. It scores four points.

Tunnel The space formed between the legs of the two front lines in the *scrum*.

Shane Goble outpaces the opposition to plant the ball for a try. Tries are the focal point of rugby, and each team should be determined to end each period of possession with a try. There is an advantage in grounding the ball as close to the goal as possible, because it makes the kick for conversion much easier.

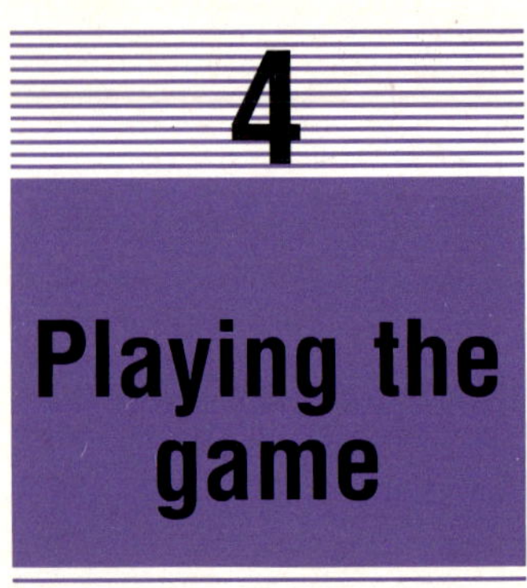

4 Playing the game

The game is controlled by a single referee, assisted by two touch-judges, one on each side of the field.

Rugby matches are divided into two halves, with a half-time interval of up to five minutes. The teams change ends at half-time. In senior matches, the maximum duration of each half is forty minutes. Shorter periods of play are normally used in junior matches. The referee will add time to take into account play lost due to injury or other stoppages, including what he judges to be time-wasting.

Before the game starts the two captains toss a coin. The winner of the toss can then choose whether to kick off, or which goal to defend. The match is started by a kick-off from the centre of the field.

The ball must be kicked *forwards*; you cannot pass it sideways as in soccer. Any player may kick off, but the task is often given to the fly-half. The ball has to cross the opponents' 10-metre line. Assuming that the kick-off is satisfactory, any player who is *onside* (not offside) may at any time:

- catch or pick up the ball and run with it
- pass the ball to another player
- kick the ball
- tackle a player holding the ball
- fall on the ball
- participate in a scrum, ruck, maul or line-out

... provided he does not break any of the laws of the game in doing so.

As soon as the player taking the kick-off contacts the ball, it is "in play", and the object of both teams must be to gain possession and score as soon as possible. This involves the use of a lot of muscle, and the generation of a lot of energy and passion. Played enthusiastically, rugby is a tough game, and occasional bruises are inevitable. However, woven into the laws of the game are many regulations which are designed to keep the dangers within acceptable limits.

Out of play from a kick-off
There are several ways the ball may go out of play from a kick-off, and each can have a different effect on the game. Here are some typical examples you may see:

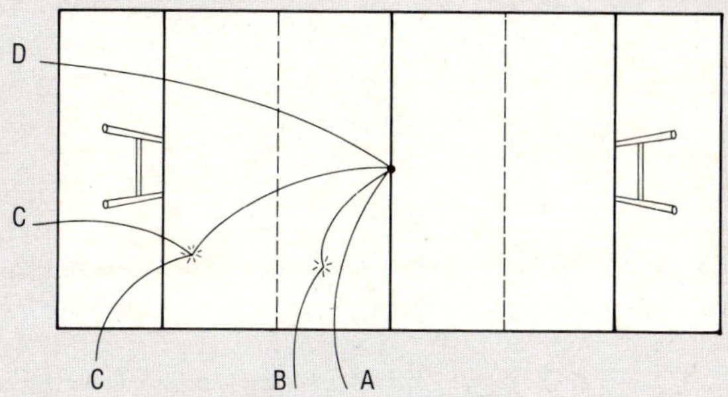

Figure 3 Out of play from a kick-off

A *The ball goes straight to touch without bouncing.* The defending team can:

- accept the kick, in which case a line-out is held at the halfway line
- ask for the kick to be taken again
- accept a scrum at the centre of the halfway line, into which they put the ball.

B *The ball goes into touch after bouncing on the field.* This is a normal kick to touch, and a line-out is held where touch was made.

C *The ball bounces and then passes over the goal line before going out of play.* In this case the defending team takes a drop-out from their 22-metre line.

D *The ball is kicked directly over the dead-ball line.* Here the defending team again has a choice:

- to accept the kick, in which case they take a drop-out from their 22-metre line
- to ask for the kick to be taken again
- to accept a scrum at the centre, into which they put the ball.

Let's take a look at the main components of play, and see how to perform them successfully and safely:

Tackling

A player with the ball is *tackled* if he is *held* and brought to the ground, or allows the ball to touch the ground. The *holding* is the important part – it is not enough just to knock over, or trip up, the opponent. A player who has been correctly tackled must release the ball at once, if he hasn't managed to pass it on the way down. Even under the pressures of a tackle, the ball must not be allowed to go forwards; if it does, it is a *knock-on*.

Dos and don'ts of the tackle

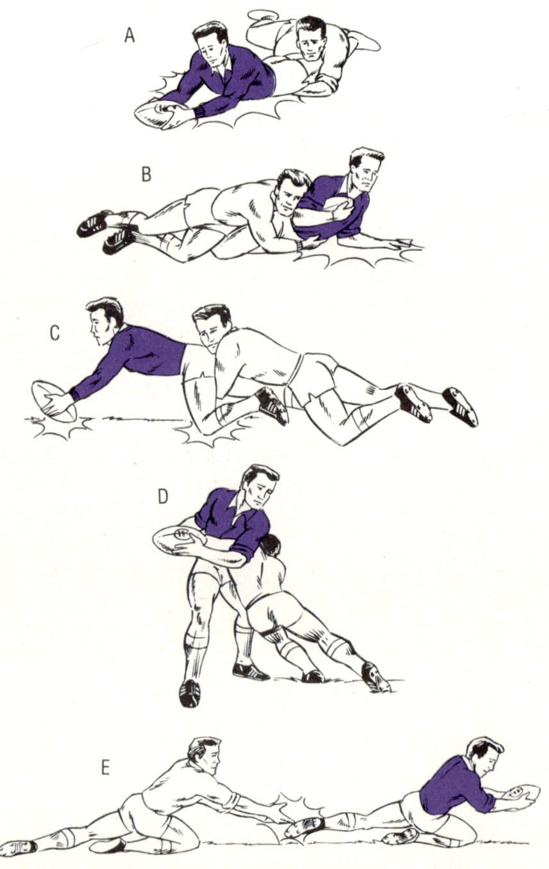

Figure 4 A, B and C are all valid tackles, because the player with the ball is held, and either he (B and C) or the ball (A and C) is on the ground. D and E are not valid tackles; D because neither the player with the ball nor the ball itself is on the ground, and E because the player is not held.

John Buckton on the receiving end of a classic flying tackle

Handing-off The player with the ball is allowed to push opponents away with his open hand. Only a pushing action is permitted: there must be no striking or punching.

Down or not? If the player with the ball is off his feet and *held*, with a knee on the ground, he is tackled, and must release the ball. Similarly, if he ends up on top of the tackler or another player who is on the ground, the tackle still counts.

Scoring when tackled If the tackled player was close to the goal-line, and manages to ground the ball on it or over it, a try may be given if the referee considers that the player's momentum took him to the line.

Players on the ground A player on the ground is not allowed to play the ball or to attempt to hang on to it. You must get up before resuming play. This applies in all situations throughout the game except for the act of actually scoring a try. In this case, the try must be scored immediately – it's no use thinking that the referee will let you get away with crawling over the line!

Tackling skills

Good tackling calls for lots of courage and determination, but timing and technique are also vital. Confidence is the key, and the best way to build this is through constant contact practice during training.

The key elements of a good tackle are:

- Be positive! Start fast, but take care to arrive in balance to avoid being easily beaten by your opponent.

- Before making the tackle, try to run your opponent into a position from which he cannot easily dodge.
- Aim to hit with your shoulder just above your opponent's knees.
- Ensure that your head is *behind* his thighs to avoid getting hurt when he falls.
- Grip your opponent tightly by swinging your arms right around his thighs.
- Get your opponent to the ground by driving powerfully with your legs.

The majority of tackles are from the side, but you must also be prepared to attack from the front or the back. If you wish to prevent the player with the ball from passing it, you may have to use a smother tackle: in this you use your body to cover the ball while grabbing your opponent.

Resisting a tackle

Obviously, if you can evade the tackle by weaving or handing-off, so much the better. However, as soon as you meet the tackle, you can try to "buy time" by remaining on your feet as long as possible, so that your team-mates can get into position for an effective pass. With the right sort of support, there is often the opportunity to set up fresh attacking possibilities. As soon as hitting the ground becomes inevitable, try to place the ball so that your team can retain possession.

The scrum

A scrum is the method used to re-start the game after a variety of stoppages. The forwards bind together, and push against the opposing team, head-to-head. The ball is placed between the feet of the players in the front rows, and each team tries to channel it backwards so that it emerges in a position where their link-players (scrum-half or fly-half) can pass it to the backs to continue the attack.

There is an advantage for the team which puts the ball into the scrum, so this is done by the scrum-half of the side which did *not* cause the stoppage.

The laws of the scrum state that:

- A scrum must be formed by at least five players from each side. Eight is normal – teams rarely form a scrum with fewer.
- Players must bind tightly together.
- Players will be penalised if they take up a position that is likely to cause the scrum to collapse.

The forwards prepare to lock the scrum together

- The ball must be played with the feet only, unless the scrum has moved into the in-goal area.
- Once the ball has emerged from the scrum, it must not be put in again unless ordered by the referee. (This is normally done only if it comes out of either end of the tunnel.)

The ball has taken the wrong path out of the scrum, because the forwards haven't controlled it effectively: this has left the scrum-half a lot to do!

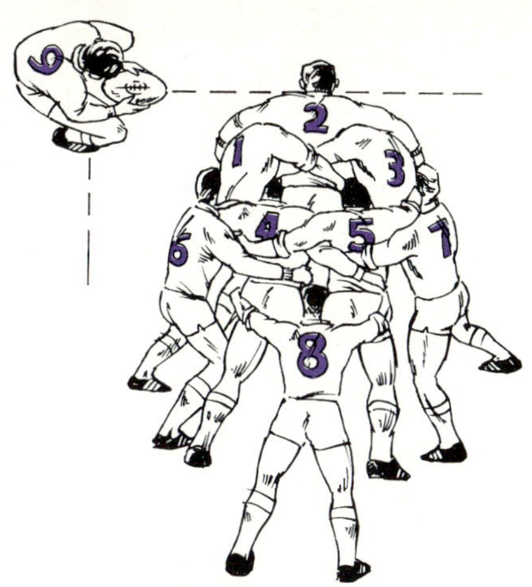

Figure 5 How a team packs together for the scrum

When the scrum-half puts the ball into the scrum, he must:

- stand one metre away, midway between the opposing front rows
- hold the ball in both hands, between knee and ankle
- put the ball in without delay (no "dummying"), along the centre line of the scrum, to touch the ground in the tunnel

The front row forwards are not allowed to lift their feet until the ball has touched ground in the tunnel.

Safety in the scrum
There is a danger of injury during a collapse of the scrum, so the following rules are strictly enforced in the players' interests:

- Players' shoulders must not be lower than their hips.
- A player in the front row must not raise both feet off the ground at the same time (this used to be a favourite ploy used by hookers to get the ball).
- Players must not contribute to the collapse of the scrum in any way. This includes pulling an opponent's clothing, twisting, or deliberately kicking the ball out along the tunnel.
- There must never be more than three players in the front row: players who attempt to add themselves to the front three will be penalised.

This scrum has collapsed into a tangled mass of forwards as the scrum-half gets the ball away with a deft pivot pass

Offside rules around the scrum

At scrums, rucks and mauls, a player is offside if he is in front of the offside line, which is an imaginary line running parallel to the goal lines and through the rearmost foot on his side of the scrum, ruck or maul. This is the case whether he runs over the line or merely finds himself there. An offside player will be penalised if he attempts to play the ball or impede an opponent.

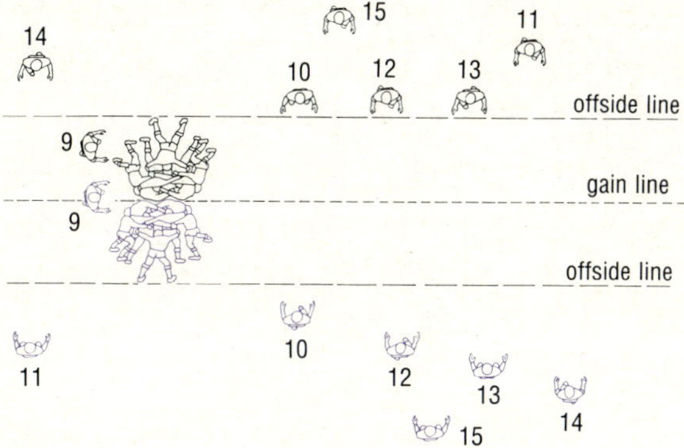

Figure 6 The offside lines at the scrum

The ruck

A ruck is a form of scrum which develops when the ball is on the ground and players from both sides gather around it and push for possession. Because a ruck is formed by the will of the players rather than at the direction of the referee, it can be rather an untidy affair, but *the same rules of behaviour apply as for a formal scrum.*

The maul

A maul occurs when a number of players gather around one who is holding the ball. A frequent response is to drop the ball onto the ground, when the maul immediately becomes a ruck.

The line-out

A line-out is the method used to re-start play when the ball goes off the field and *into touch*, by contacting or crossing over the touchlines, or landing on the ground outside them. This can happen if the ball is kicked over the line, or if the player carrying it is forced onto the line or over it. Because the line-out is usually taken

The lines of forwards shield their eyes from slanting winter sunlight as the ball is thrown into the line-out. In this case the striped team's number 8 is throwing the ball; it is more usual for the hooker (number 2) to throw in.

at the point on the touchline where the ball went into touch, it can be an effective way of making ground. However, you must be sure that you understand the rules for putting the ball into touch correctly (see page 31) before kicking wildly at the touchline!

The rules of the line-out

A line-out is formed by at least two players from each side (usually seven), who line up in single lines, parallel to each other and at right-angles to the touchline.

- The ball is thrown in by a player from the team which did not contact the ball last.
- The team throwing the ball in determines the maximum number of players who can take part in the line-out.
- The line-out takes place between the 5-metre and 15-metre lines which run parallel with the touchlines. Any player who is outside these lines is not considered to be taking part in the line-out.
- Players on the same side must stand one metre apart, and the two lines must be at least half a metre apart.
- Jostling and shoving in the line-out is not allowed. Until the ball has touched one of the players in the line-out, they must all remain the required distance apart unless they are in the act of jumping for the

ball. Movements to jump or catch must not be made until the ball has left the thrower's hands.

- The player throwing the ball in must keep both feet behind the touchline. He may throw with one or both hands.
- Any player can throw the ball in: it was once normal for the wing-threequarter to do it, but nowadays it is common for one of the forwards (normally the hooker) to throw, leaving the line of attacking backs unbroken.

Offside rules in the line-out

The offside rules in the line-out are very complicated, and often confusing for beginners.

First, let's get clear about who counts as being part of the line-out:

- The two lines of players (usually forwards)
- The player who is throwing the ball, and his opposite number
- One other player from each side, who is in position to receive the ball; these are normally the scrum-halves

Players who are in the line-out

Any of these participating players can become offside in various situations:

- If a player moves over the line of touch (except when actually jumping for the ball) before the ball has touched a player or the ground, he is offside.

Hotly disputed possession in the line-out

- Once the ball has touched a player or the ground, a player who is not carrying the ball must not get ahead of the ball except to correctly tackle an opponent in the line-out; if he does, he is offside.
- You are not allowed to "peel off": you must stay close to the line-out until it has ended or until you have joined a ruck or maul which has formed from it.
- You must not go more than 15 metres from the touchline, except to receive a long throw-in – and if you do, your opponents are allowed to follow you. It has to be a member of your team who throws the ball in, and you must not exceed the 15 metres until the ball has left his hands. Judge the long throw-in carefully: if the ball fails to reach you, you will end up offside anyway!

Players who are not in the line-out
All players who are not part of the line-out must be behind the offside line. This is an imaginary line drawn 10 metres back from the line of touch (see Figure 7). Any such player who is ahead of this line is offside. If the line of touch is less than 10 metres from the goal-line, the offside line is the goal-line.

There is an exception which again involves a long throw-in. In this case, you can go beyond the offside line to receive the ball, once it has left your team-mate's hands; if you do this, your opponents are allowed to advance to meet you. Again, if you misjudge the length of the throw, and it doesn't reach you, you will be offside.

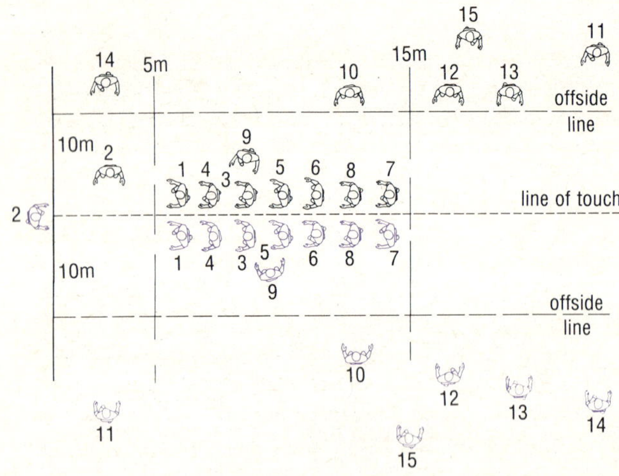

Figure 7 Offside in the line-out

Touch and the touchlines

The touchlines are the outer boundaries of the field of play, so the ball only has to touch them to go "into touch". Similarly, it is in touch if a player carrying the ball touches the line with just the tip of his boot.

The rules for kicking to touch in open play (that is, not from penalties or free-kicks) are:

1 A player will gain ground if he kicks directly to touch from within his 22-metre area – the ball does not need to bounce first.

2 A player kicking into touch from outside his 22-metre area must make the ball bounce in the field of play before it crosses the touchline, if he is to gain ground. If he kicks directly to touch without a bounce, the resulting line-out is taken level with the point at which the ball was kicked, or (if it happens to cross the touchline nearer his own goal line) at the point where it crossed the line.

3 From a free-kick or a penalty, the ball may be kicked directly into touch, and the line-out is taken from where it crossed the line.

It is an offence for the ball to be *thrown* into touch deliberately: a penalty kick is awarded against a player who does this.

If there is a strong wind blowing across the pitch, it is not unusual for the ball to cross the line while in the air, but then to be blown back onto the pitch before touching anything. In this case, it is not considered to have "made touch", and play continues normally.

Jumping for the ball as the black team's hooker throws in. The opposing backs are seen lined across the field ready to advance if their team gains possession.

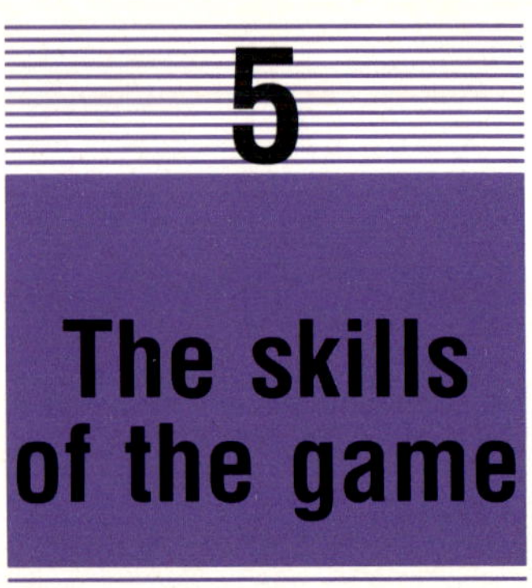

5 The skills of the game

A rugby ball is not a complicated piece of equipment, but it behaves in unpredictable ways. It will bounce very differently, according to whether it lands on end or sideways, and seems never to go the way you want it to. You have to master this odd behaviour, and there is no substitute for practice. Aim at using your spare time to perfect your skill with the ball.

Handling

Picking up

Learn to pick the ball up cleanly at speed. It should soon become instinctive to approach alongside, bend your knees and scoop the ball up in one smooth action.

Holding

Whenever you can, hold the ball with both hands, one each side of its middle. This seems pretty obvious, but it is surprising how often possession is lost through trying to hold or throw with one hand. Remember that if the ball is held between your hand and your body, you cannot move its position rapidly in response to a challenge.

Falling on the ball

When you cannot pick the ball up because the opposition is too close, you may have to fall on it – important because it denies the ball to the opposition and often prevents certain try-scoring situations from developing. The trick is to fall with your back to the opposition and to use your whole body to guard the ball as you go down. But remember, you are not allowed to huddle round the ball and stay there: you must immediately get to your feet with the ball. If you can't gather it up, you must release it on the ground and roll away from it.

Determined running on the mini-rugby pitch

Running

Practise running with the ball; get used to moving fast with it under either arm, as well as holding it in both hands. Run with determination to beat the opposition! Don't just practise straight lines – develop the evasion skills of side-step, swerve and change of pace.

You can practise some of these skills on your own, but there is no real substitute for setting up realistic routines with your team-mates. Sharpen up your tactics and decision-making by taking it in turns to represent the opposition.

Passing

Youngsters often find it difficult to understand the concept "run forwards but pass backwards". Rugby is simply a game where you run forward with the ball, but when challenged, you transfer it to a team-mate who is further from the opposing goal-line. Of course, the receiving player does not have to be directly behind; provided the referee is satisfied that he is not actually ahead, he can be as far to one side or the other as you like. For this reason, the typical pass is sideways and a little way backwards.

To make your passing effective, remember to:

- *Hold the ball in both hands.* This is so that you can pass to left or right without delay.
- *Turn your head and look at your target.* Too many mistakes are made by throwing the ball vaguely in the right direction and hoping for the best.
- *Throw towards your team-mate's chest.* This improves his chances of taking the ball safely.

- *Throw smoothly, using your arms, wrists and fingers.* A jerked flick of the ball will lack power and accuracy.
- *Follow the pass.* Support the player you have passed to – he may need help.

When you are receiving the pass, you can improve your chances of success by:

- *Providing a good target.* When receiving, you should reach towards the ball with both hands, ready to take the ball early.
- *Watch the ball.* Don't be distracted – watch the ball all the way into your hands.

- *Keep the ball a bit away from your body.* If you pull it tight into your body, you will not be able to accelerate away as quickly, or pass it on as rapidly.
- *Be ready to pass it on.* Try to develop the skill of knowing where the nearest players in your team are, and get the ball to the one with the best chance of making ground.
- *Run forward!* As soon as you have the ball, run straight for the goal-line. Don't waste time and give the opposition the chance to re-group by running sideways across the field.

Scrum-half passing specialities

The scrum-half probably gets more opportunities to pass than any of the other players, and has to use a number of different passes. As well as the orthodox running pass, he should also be a master of the pass *off-the-ground*, and the *pivot* and *dive* passes.

Off-the-ground pass

A good scrum-half will develop the technique of passing the ball off the ground straight to the backs. The method is to step past the ball with your front foot, bringing your back foot close up to it. Now bend your knees and sweep the ball off the ground. Your fingers should be spread quite wide when you do this. Now follow through, keeping low. It should all become one fluid action, and you will end up in a running crouch, with your front foot pointing straight at the receiver.

Pivot pass

This is similar to the orthodox pass, but you pivot on the leading foot in order to aim at the receiver.

Dive pass

This is another pass in which ball is collected from the ground and passed straight on. You approach the ball from behind, directly in line with the receiver: get your feet close to the ball, and sweep it up and throw it with a dive towards him. You will end the sequence flat on the ground. For the pass to be effective, it is essential that you know just where your team-mate is before you scoop up the ball. You must also keep your eyes on him throughout the action. The dive pass is an essential weapon in the armoury of any scrum-half.

A dive pass perfectly timed to elude the opposition

The switch pass

Also called the *scissors*, this pass is part of a routine which is designed to wrong-foot the opposition and change the angle of attack. Imagine that you have the ball and are running down the left-hand 15-metre line, with the winger on your left. Accelerate slightly to the left, across the front of your winger; the opposition will imagine that you are going for the corner flag, but as you run in front of the winger, you hand the ball to him with a short pass. The action should be gentle and undramatic. The opposition will be directing their efforts towards chasing you to the corner flag, and valuable moments will have been gained for your winger to go for the line unopposed.

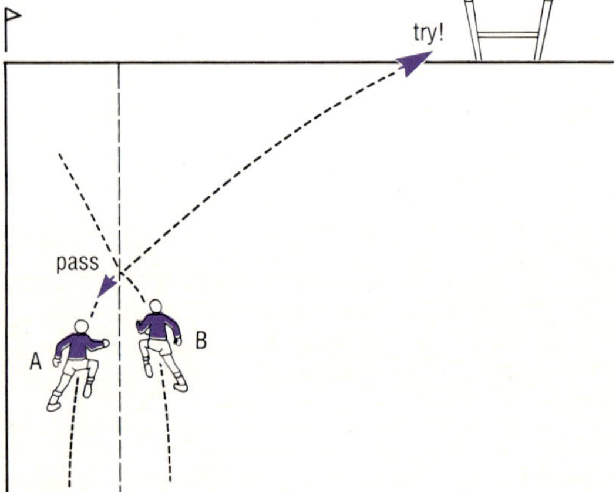

Figure 8 The switch pass: B passes the ball to A where their paths cross

The dummy pass

One of the most satisfying passing actions is not actually a pass at all! The *dummy pass* is designed to make the opposition think you are going to do one thing, while you actually do another.

The dummy can be used in many ways, but without practice and quick thinking it is useless. All it really consists of is going through the actions of a real pass, right up to the point where you would release the ball. The opposition instinctively follows what they assume to be the path of the ball, and you belt off up the field unopposed. That's the theory, anyway, and it really does work. It's no good being half-hearted about "selling the dummy". The start of the pass has to be done with true conviction if you are going to fool anybody. It is seen at its most effective when performed quite instinctively by a skilled player.

If the ball is wet and slippery with mud, watch that a planned dummy pass doesn't turn into the real thing!

The screen pass

This pass is used to protect the ball in tight situations, when you are under threat from one or more opponents. Rather than going to the ground still in possession, run straight at your opponent and at the moment of impact, drop your shoulder and half-turn your body. This protects the ball as you drive on, and you then make a very short pass to a team-mate. Naturally this is only possible if you are receiving close back-up.

Passing checklist

- Never pass forwards, but don't be afraid to pass sideways and only slightly backwards.
- Pass while you are still in control.
- Be ready to receive the ball safely by providing a good target.
- Practise all the different kinds of pass.

Kicking

So far we have concentrated on rugby as a *handling* game; however, it is also a *kicking* game. Kicking plays an important part in rugby in a variety of ways: it is an option in attack, it can bring relief in defence, and it can gain points when kicking at goal.

When kicking is done well it can be very effective, but too often young players use it aimlessly, without thought or direction. Kicking needs to be *practised*, and players should know the *purpose* of the kick:

- *why* kick?
- *which* kick?
- *where* to kick?

Remember, you cannot *throw* the ball forward, and you cannot *pass* it forward, but you are allowed to *kick* it forward, and there are times when this can be very useful.

Kicks out of *defence* are usually to relieve pressure from the opposition – to take play away from your own goal-line and back into your opponents' territory. Defensive kicks do not have to be into touch; they can be booted straight down the middle of the field, especially if there is a strong wind behind the kicker. This forces the opposition to decide whether to kick the ball back down the field or to attempt to run with it. Whatever they choose, you will have gained valuable time. The pressure will be off your goal-line, and you will be able to regroup, even though you have lost possession. If the other team decide to kick into touch, your possession may not be lost for long, because the throw-in goes to your team, which gives you the advantage.

Kicks in attack need thought: the advantage of putting the ball behind the opposing defence may be outweighed by the fact that you will almost certainly lose possession. Kicks in attack should either be *high*, or into *vacant space*, so that your side has a good chance of regaining possession and going on to score.

Time spent perfecting your kicking will not be wasted. Whatever type of kick you make, be sure to keep your head down and your eyes on the ball. Always complete the action with a smooth follow-through.

Here are the different types of kick, with an indication of when and where to use them:

Place-kick

As the name suggests, the ball is placed on the ground and kicked from there. Used at the halfway line, this is the kick which starts the match, and re-starts it after the interval. The place-kick is also the normal way of

No doubt about the follow-through from this place-kick. Note how the player has kept his head steady and his eyes on the ball.

making a conversion from a try, which calls for great power and accuracy, particularly when the try has been made towards the touchline.

Although the laws allow it, the place-kick is not used when taking a free-kick, as the opposing team is allowed to run for the ball as soon as it is placed on the ground.

It is now usual to take a place-kick with the ball upright. Make your run-up brisk but controlled, and paced so that it brings your non-kicking foot just along-side the ball. You must aim to hit the ball with the top of your kicking foot, which should contact it just below its centre. This style of place-kick calls for your foot to be pointed down from the ankle, which should be braced firm as you make contact. A good follow-through finishes the kick. If the follow-through is not automatic, then you are not putting as much fluid effort into the kick as it demands!

Drop-kick

A drop-kick is mainly used to score a goal during play, or to score from a penalty. The ability to drop-kick reliably is a very useful skill for all rugby players.

Drop-kicking is deceptively simple: you drop the ball just in front of you, pointed end downwards, and then your foot hits the ball just as it bounces. The trick is in the timing, and there is no substitute for plenty of practice to get this right. As with the place-kick, contact is usually made with the top of the foot, adjusting the angle according to whether height or distance is required.

The punt

This is the kick most frequently used during the normal flow of the game. It can be a powerful kick for distance, perhaps when trying to find touch a long way into your opponents' half, or it may be a short kick into a vacant space on the field. The punt which goes a short distance before rolling along the ground for one of your team-mates to pick up is traditionally called a "grubber".

The punt is simpler than the drop-kick because the ball goes straight from hand to boot, without having to bounce. For maximum distance, contact the ball with the upper part of your foot, almost towards your ankle. To kick a *grubber*, or to make a short but high chip-shot over the opposition, again use the top of your foot, but much nearer the toe. Alter the angle of the foot according to how much height you need.

The punt should be a tactical kick. Use it:

- In defence: winning time to regroup by sending the ball a long way up the field or into touch.

- In attack: as a *cross-kick*, for your backs to gather and press on with; as an *up-and-under*, where it is kicked high to give time for your fellow-attackers to run underneath; as the delicately named *grubber*, skittering along the ground just behind the defence; or as a *chip*, lightly kicked over your opponents' heads and falling just behind them.

Dribbling

Dribbling a rugby ball along the ground is almost a forgotten art. Keeping the ball close to your feet and under control is not at all easy, as you will no doubt find out! However, it is worth persevering with practice, because the skill can be very effective, particularly in muddy conditions when it is too difficult to pick up a slippery ball. It is fortunate that under these conditions the mud tends to have a damping effect on the uneven bounce of the ball.

Whatever type of kick you are making, it is important to keep your head down, and keep your eyes on the ball until after it has been kicked.

Penalty kick and free-kick

The main difference between these two kicks is that you can score direct from a penalty, but not from a free-kick. As a general rule the referee awards free-kicks against minor technical offences and penalties against more serious ones. Here is a short summary of the rules:

Law 27 Penalty kick

A penalty kick is given to the non-offending side after major infringement. Any player from that side may:

1 kick for goal
2 kick for touch
3 take a tap penalty

When the penalty is taken, the rest of the side must be behind the ball when it is kicked. The offending side must retire 10 metres from the mark.

Law 17 Free-kick

This is normally awarded for technical offences at scrum and line-outs – as for penalty but:

1 A kick at goal is not allowed.
2 The opposing players may charge the ball as soon as the kicker places the ball on the ground or begins his run to kick.

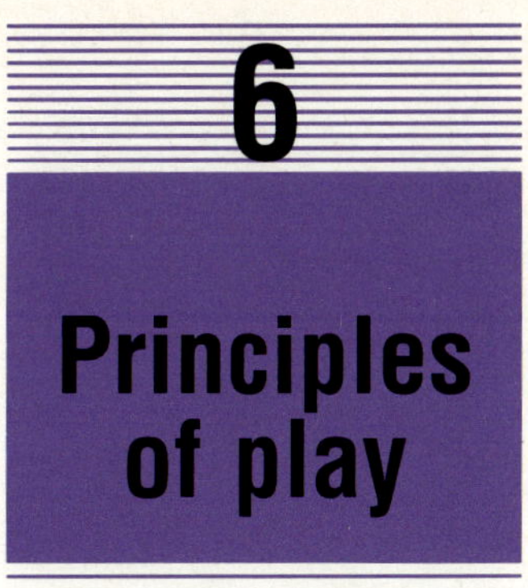

6 Principles of play

Rugby is a team game, and cooperation is necessary if your team is to win. You cannot possibly know all the techniques or have mastered all the skills at the beginning of your playing career, but you can understand the broad principles. If you keep the following points in mind every time you walk out onto the field, you will be off to a good start!

- *If you've got the ball, go forwards* – not backwards or sideways. It is the responsibility of the player with the ball to get it ahead of the rest of his team.
- *Anticipate the tackles.* Learn to predict where you will meet an opponent by understanding the tackle line. This is an imaginary line across the field indicating the points where opposing players will meet. The position of the tackle line depends on the speed, reaction, and starting positions of both the attacking and the defending sides.

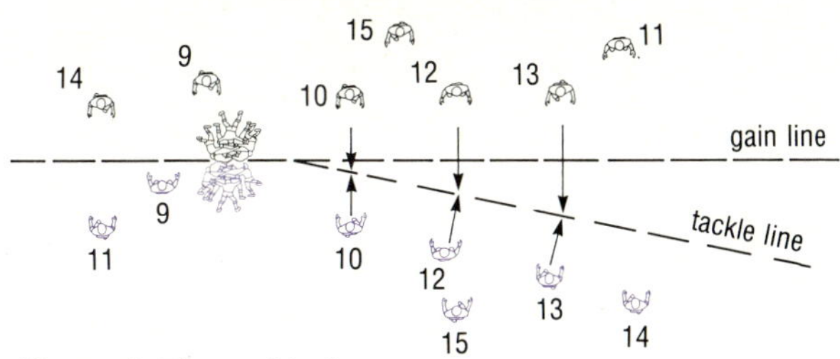

Figure 9 The tackle line

- *Do all you can to get and keep possession.* The side without the ball cannot score. Never let up in your attempts to secure possession from all phases of play – at scrums, line-outs, rucks, mauls and tackles.
- *In open play, everyone can be a ball-winner:* backs, as well as forwards, should be able to ruck and maul.

Strong support by England against France

- *In support.* Build the ability to "read the game" and to run intelligently in support of the player with the ball. Seek out where the opposition is thinnest and try to run into that vacant space. Try to be part of a support group in the form of a deep wedge of players formed directly behind the player on the attack. Shallow support (to the side of the player with the ball) is less effective.
- *In defence.* You can still attack even if you don't have the ball. Run at the opponent with the ball – this denies him time and space. He is put under pressure and therefore likely to make a mistake.
- Disrupt the opposing side if they seem likely to get possession. The side that puts the ball into the scrum is the one most likely to gain possession. At such times you must do all you can to disrupt the possession. Keep shoving – a scrum going backwards can't control the ball effectively!
- *Make support instinctive:* think where you need to be to assist a player if he runs into trouble, and *be there.* The closer you make your support, the more likely your side will be to retain possession.
- *Keep the pressure on:* take the game to the opposition in both attack and defence – deny them time and space. A team under pressure often makes mistakes, giving opportunities to score points or regain possession.
- *Keep the pace up,* both in running and in thinking. A side playing at a good pace puts the opposition under pressure and therefore makes them vulnerable.

- *Be ready to adjust.* Be prepared for the extra effort you will have to make as you move up into higher-standard teams. Many players promoted from club to county level have admitted that they have found it difficult to adapt because of the extra pace of the game – everything happens so much more quickly.

Stopping and starting

There are many reasons why play stops in rugby, and quite a number of different ways of starting again. The following points are the *main* reasons for stopping, and the *usual* method for the corresponding re-start. As with all matters concerning control of the game, it is the referee who decides exactly how the game proceeds at any time, and his word must be accepted *without question.* Discussion on his interpretation of the law can take place after the game!

Kick-off

A place-kick from the centre of the halfway line is used to start each half and to re-start play after a successful kick at goal (Law 10). The ball must travel 10 metres. The kick must not take the ball out of play without bouncing (see page 21): if that should happen, the opposing side may choose for the kick-off to be retaken or for a scrum to be formed at the halfway line, with their scrum-half putting the ball in.

After a knock-on or throw forward

If the knock-on (see page 16) is unintentional, the referee will award a scrum with the non-offending side putting the ball in. If he thinks the act was intentional he will award a penalty to the nonoffending side. The scrum or penalty will be taken from the point where the offence occurred (Law 17).

After a tackle

As soon as the player carrying the ball is held by an opponent, and at the same time is brought to the ground or the ball touches the ground, he must release it (not in a forward direction). Play continues, but players on the ground must not attempt to play the ball until they are back on their feet.

After an offside offence

A penalty kick is awarded to the other side (Law 24).

When the ball goes into touch

A throw-in (line-out) occurs at the point where the ball crossed or touched the line. The throw is taken by the side which did not last touch the ball.

After a try has been scored

A place-kick at goal is taken. This can be from anywhere on the pitch, in line with the point at which the try was made.

After a conversion

A place-kick is taken from the centre of the halfway line, by the side which did not score.

When the ball goes over the dead-ball line

There are two ways this is dealt with:

- If the *attacking* side sent the ball over, the defending team takes a drop-kick from behind their 22-metre line.
- If the *defending* team is responsible, then the game is re-started with a scrum 5 metres from the try line, in line with the point where the ball went over it. The attacking team puts the ball into the scrum.

Always remember the advantage rule (see page 14). Simply "play to the whistle", and do not stop if the opposition infringes the laws unless the referee blows his whistle.

John Buckton, the Yorkshire and Saracens centre-back, gets his pass away just as he is tackled

7 Kit and equipment

There is an old saying that "a smart team is not necessarily a good team, but good teams always look smart".

If you are going to play rugby, you might as well get used to the idea that mud is part of the game, and your kit will need washing after every match: don't roll it up and leave it in the bag for a couple of days. Similarly, your boots must be dried out very slowly and cleaned thoroughly between games. Several generations of rugby players have conned their wives, mothers and sweethearts into accepting responsibility for doing the washing, but the boots are definitely something that the players do for themselves!

Clothing

Rugby kit has become fairly standardised, and as in many other athletic sports, the choice is between cotton and synthetics. Choose cotton or a cotton mixture every time, because it will absorb sweat readily. Shirts and shorts take quite a lot of punishment, so go for good quality with reinforced seams, if you can afford it.

Your socks should be in your school or club colours if you can possibly afford it. The type with a looped pile are particularly comfortable.

Trunks or underpants are a must under your shorts.

A tracksuit is a worthwhile investment too: wear it as you warm up for training, and to stop getting chilled if there is any waiting around afterwards.

Many clubs with a youth section operate a second-hand kit scheme so that young players can easily pass on outgrown kit. Once you graduate to playing for a club's senior teams, you may find that shirts and shorts are provided.

Boots

Your boots are probably the most important item of kit, and you need to choose them carefully. It is usual for backs to wear fairly lightweight boots of the soccer type, while some forwards use true rugby boots which give some support around the ankles. In either case, buy one size larger than your usual shoe size, and wear an extra pair of socks – this will help prevent blisters.

If you go for soccer-type footwear, you can often make a worthwhile saving by buying boots bearing the name of a once-famous footballer who is no longer very popular (there's no shortage of these!). Usually the unfashionable name is the only thing wrong with an otherwise excellent pair of boots which are being sold cheaply.

Whatever boots you choose, make sure that the studs comply with the regulations (see panel).

After a match it is very easy to remember the highlights and to forget about boring matters like cleaning your boots. However, they do need extra-special care: wash off excess mud and allow them to dry naturally (don't put them on the stove or in an airing cupboard). A good tip is to stuff them with old newspapers as soon as you can, then leave them for a day or two. This will absorb moisture and help to maintain their shape. Polish or dubbin them well when dry.

Don't wear boots that have a single stud at the toe.

Do wear boots with studs that conform to British Standard BS6366:1983. Studs *must* be circular, securely fastened and have the following sizes:

Length (maximum)	18 mm
Diameter at base (minimum)	13 mm
Diameter at top (minimum)	10 mm
Min. diameter of integral washer	20 mm

A referee will prevent you from playing if your studs are in a dangerous condition. Plastic studs are normally banned. Moulded rubber multi-studded soles are acceptable.

Other equipment

Shin guards are very important for players in the front five of the scrum. The guards are usually made of light but strong plastic, and the edges must be rounded and smooth. Most players prefer to wear them in between two pairs of socks.

Players in the scrum may also decide to use a

Studs are essential for traction: six-stud and eight-stud patterns are seen here.

headband to protect their ears. Make sure that anything like this that you use has no buckles which may damage you or anyone else.

A gum shield or mouth guard is essential protection for your teeth (see page 49).

After the match, a bath or shower is essential, so don't forget your towel and any toiletries you prefer.

Lastly, use a bag or holdall *with your name on it* to keep all your kit together. Be methodical about preparing your kit and packing it before a match – there's nothing more unsettling than arriving for an away fixture and discovering that your boots are still at home.

Rugby ball

A rugby ball is not essential, but if you have the chance to get one, you will find that it can be a great help when practising with your friends in your spare time. You will learn faster if you use a ball of a size that suits you. There are three sizes: six- to nine-year-olds need the smallest, size 3; ten to thirteens need size 4, while older teenagers should use size 5, the full-size ball.

The rules for the full-size ball (size 5) are as follows:

The ball should be oval in shape, with four panels, and of the following dimensions:

length in line	280–300 mm
circumference (A)	760–790 mm
circumference (B)	580–620 mm

B
A

The ball should be inflated to a pressure of between 9½ and 10 pounds per square inch.

Safety in play

Rugby is a rough and robust game, but it need not be a dangerous one. Most of the points we give here are matters of common sense, and apply equally to any other fairly vigorous activity:

- Play according to the rules at all times. Many of them have been introduced for the protection of the players – a typical example is the rule that shoulders must be above the level of the hips during all forms of scrum activity, so that there is little danger of collapse.
- *Never* chew gum or suck sweets while playing rugby, or while taking part in any other sport. You can easily choke on the gum during play, and this could be very dangerous if you were to be knocked unconscious, as the gum could "go down the wrong way" and obstruct breathing.
- Cuts, scrapes and grazes occur frequently, so do have a course of anti-tetanus injections. Your doctor will advise you on these.
- Always warm up thoroughly before training and matches.
- Learn the correct technique for contact situations. Don't hurl yourself into the game with more enthusiasm than technique: learn how to fall onto the ball; to tackle; to handle scrums, rucks and mauls.
- Make sure you are physically capable of playing the game. The fitter you are, the less likely you are to suffer an injury.
- Do not allow children to take part in weight-training or resistance exercises. These should not be introduced until the mid- to late teens, when the bone structure is fully developed.

- Always play to the *spirit* of the game: good sportsmanship is a long-established and accepted tradition with both players and spectators. The game is hard and uncompromising, but *fair*.

Safety in dress

- *Do not* wear dangerous projections, such as buckles, rings, necklaces, watches or earrings.
- *Do* protect your teeth by wearing a gum shield or mouth guard. See your dentist for advice early on – don't wait until you have received an accidental boot in the face!
- *Do* wear shin guards if you are one of the front five forwards.

Treatment of injury

Concussion

The RFU make an emphatic recommendation: "A player who has suffered definite concussion should not participate in any match or training session for a period of at least three weeks from the time of the injury, and then only subject to being cleared by a proper neurological examination." There's no arguing with that!

Soft-tissue injuries

Even with very good warm-up routines and care in play, in a contact sport like rugby there will inevitably be some injuries to muscles, tendons and ligaments. If the injury appears at all serious, get proper medical attention at once. However, minor injuries can be given the "RICE" treatment:

Rest Stop using the injured part – if you don't rest it, permanent damage may result.

Ice Apply ice, through a plastic bag or cloth, to the injured area for 10 to 20 minutes. This will cause the blood vessels and tissues to contract, restricting the blood flow and reducing the swelling. Repeat every three hours if necessary.

Compression Keep swelling to a minimum by wrapping an elastic or crêpe bandage around the area. This can be placed over the ice-pack if necessary. Take care not to bind the bandage too tightly.

Elevation Raising the injured part will help excess fluid to drain from the damaged area, again reducing swelling.

9 Fitness

The benefits of reasonable fitness are very clear. A fitter player will be:

- more confident
- less prone to injury
- able to maintain skills and techniques longer
- able to work at a fast pace for longer
- able to recover more quickly after injury

Most youngsters are naturally fairly fit, but rugby is a *collision* sport, and therefore the body must be prepared to meet and withstand the physical demands of the game.

The more ambitious you become, the greater will be your emphasis on fitness. This is a personal matter, and in the end you have to set your own standards and be responsible for maintaining them. Today, our knowledge of the type of fitness required for rugby is scientifically based on years of research.

Everybody's training needs are slightly different, but all players will benefit from the routines suggested here. As you become more serious about rugby, your coach or teacher will help you develop your own fitness programme. There are four essentials, the *four Ss*:

- **S**uppleness
- **S**trength
- **S**tamina
- **S**peed

Suppleness

This is to develop *flexibility*, to extend the range of limb movement around a joint. Supple players are less liable to suffer ligament and muscle tears and strains.

You should limber up using steady stretching exercises for a minimum of ten minutes daily, and before each training session or match, sticking to the following principles:

- Warm muscles stretch more easily than cold ones, so wear warm clothing
- Relax!
- Do the exercises *steadily*: do not bounce or jerk
- Ease into each stretch position until it is tight but not painful
- Hold for between 10 and 15 seconds
- Use both sides of the body
- Keep to the order given here

Maintaining suppleness is such a good way of preventing injury that we describe the exercises in fuller detail than those for strength, stamina and speed. The numbers in brackets refer to the photographs on pages 52 and 55.

1 Neck

Drop your head forward, and slowly rotate it in a wide circle, first one way and then the other.

2 Arms, shoulders and chest

Full arm circling: stand with your back straight and trace large circles with your arms straight, brushing your ears and thighs on each rotation. Swing your arms both forwards and backwards.

Elbow pull: with your arms bent overhead, grasp one elbow with the opposite hand and gently pull the elbow behind your head: repeat with the other arm. (1)

3 Back and spine (2, 3, 4)

Rotation: lie flat, with your arms out in a "T" position. Raise your right leg and touch your left hand with the right foot: keep your shoulders and arms on the floor.

Sideways flexion: stand upright. Without leaning forward, slide your arm down the side of your leg.

Backward extension: kneel or stand, and curve your spine backwards.

4 Hips (5)

Lie flat on your back with one leg straight; grasp the other knee with both hands and pull it tight to your chest.

5 Groin (6)

Sit down with your knees and hips bent: now bring the soles of your feet together and gently pull yourself forward, pressing your elbows against your knees and bending further from the hips.

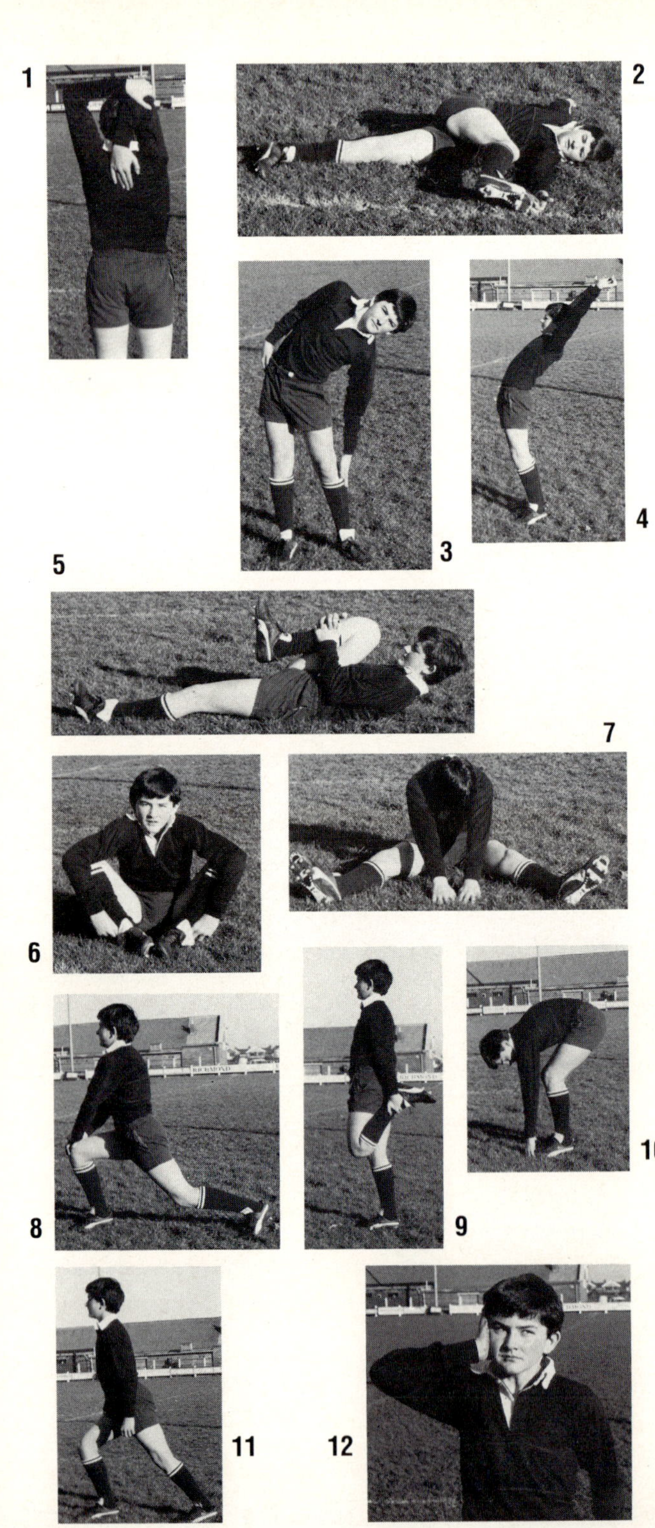

1 2 3 4 5 6 7 8 9 10 11 12

6 Groin and hips (7)
Sit with your legs as wide apart as possible, and bend forward from the hips *without bending your knees*. Do the exercise stretching your hands directly forward, and then reaching down each leg.

7 Quadriceps and hips (8)
Take up the *lunge* position as shown in the illustration, and press gently down. Perform the exercise with alternate legs forward.

8 Quadriceps (9)
Stand on one leg and pull your other ankle up against your bottom. Repeat with the other leg.

9 Hamstrings (10)
Very simple, this! Bend forward until you can stand on your fingers with your toes. Now gradually straighten your legs.

10 Calves (11)
This is similar to exercise 8, except that you must keep your feet flat on the ground. Keep straight and gently push your hips downwards.

Strength

Strength is an obvious benefit for rugby players, but young players should not put too much emphasis on it. Until the bone structure is fully developed, usually in the mid- to late teens, strength-training exercises should use only the body's resistance. Weight training is not suitable for youngsters, and should not be attempted unsupervised at any age.

Try the following strength-building exercises at least three times a week. They can all be done at home or at the rugby club. The number of repetitions of each exercise will depend on the individual, and will increase with age and fitness. Start with very small numbers and *gradually* build up.

Your training should start approximately six weeks before you start playing.

Neck

- Rotate your neck slowly as in the first suppleness exercise.
- Now add resistance by using your hand to prevent movement. (12)
- Form a bridge: lie on your back and bend your knees, keeping your feet flat on the ground. Then bend your head back and raise your bottom so that

you are supported on your feet and head only. Hold for five seconds. (13)

Shoulders and arms

It's hard to improve on the old favourites for shoulders and arms:

- *press-ups* (14)
- *pull-ups*
- *dips*
- *back press-ups*

Legs

The leg-strengthening exercises are old favourites too. These are suitable for all ages:

- *squats*: slowly, with your hands locked behind your head (15)
- *squat jumps*: from knees fully bent, to the fully extended "star" position (16)
- *step-ups*
- *hopping*
- *bunny hops*

Back and stomach

Take particular care with these exercises.

- *sit-ups*. These are demanding. They *must* be performed with your legs bent as shown: there is a risk of injury to the lower back if they are attempted with straight legs. (17)
- *leg lifts*. Lie flat on your back and raise your legs until they are vertical. Right leg, left leg, then both together. (18)
- *hip raise*. Again, lie flat on your back and attempt to raise your bottom as high as you can. (19)
- *back arches*. A real tester! Simply lie on your front, clasp your hands at the back of your neck and arch your back to raise your chest off the ground. (20)

Partner work

At rugby clubs or schools, strength training can become more enjoyable if you work with a partner.

Always use the correct technique when lifting: form a firm base, bend your legs, keep your head up and your back straight. Your legs must do the lifting, not your back. This will almost certainly prevent any injury to the spine or spinal muscles.

Try lifting your partner off the ground with your arms around his waist or under his arms; practise the "fireman's lift"; try pulling and pushing games with one

13

14

15

16

17

18

19

20

arm and both arms; push hand-to-hand, hand-to-shoulder and hand-to-head; have "two-man scrums", always remembering to keep your shoulders above your thighs. Arm-wrestling is a good strength-developer, as well as being good fun. Do it with both right and left arms, and introduce variations such as attempting to force each other's hands apart.

Stamina

Distance running is the usual way of building stamina. Start slowly, and gradually increase both speed and distance. The minimum distance you should aim at is two miles, building up to a maximum of five miles per session. Once you become confident at covering a certain distance, start to time your runs, and *keep a record of your times.* That's the only way you can measure improvement.

Speed

The player who can produce an explosive sprint when he has the ball will always do better than one who plods along, yet it is amazing how many plodders there are on rugby fields. To sprint effectively you need reasonable fitness, with good strength in your upper body as well as in your legs. You can improve on whatever natural sprinting talents you have by practising technique: try a start/stop shuttle run to sharpen up your ability to get off the mark quickly.

Shuttle run

Run 30 metres flat out; walk back; run 40 metres; walk back; run 50 metres; walk back. When this becomes too easy, add an extra sprint between the recovery walks, until you can repeat the whole routine six times. This exercise will build up stamina as well as speed.

Chain sprints

This is a mild form of torture favoured by many coaches. The team or training group are set to jog around the field. When the whistle blows, everyone has to sprint and try to overtake the player ahead, until it is blown again, when jogging resumes. This continues until the coach thinks everyone has had enough, which is usually rather longer than the runners believe they can take!

Agility sprints

Sprinting down the field around markers and over obstacles is good training for the dodging that you will need in play. Time yourself over the course, then try it again while carrying a ball.

Overall fitness

Aim at all-round fitness by eating sensibly and exercising often. Eating sensibly means eating a good variety of food which will give you the balanced mixture of protein, fats, vitamins and carbohydrate that your body needs if you are to perform efficiently on the field. Don't *always* choose chips; eat plenty of fresh fruit and vegetables; develop a taste for wholemeal bread rather than the white plastic variety. Don't imagine that because you may be a forward, it is good to be really heavy. Plenty of muscle is fine, but flab doesn't help at all.

10 Rugby for young people

In past years, children used to learn the basics of rugby by playing in the streets or playgrounds, often using a rolled-up school cap as the ball. This did not do much for the condition of the caps, but did get youngsters into the game at an early age. Now that school caps are a rarity and the streets too dangerous, this early casual experience of the game is, sadly, rather unusual. However, although unstructured games are enjoyable and exciting, they do not necessarily make you a good player: for that you need advice and instruction. You need *coaching*, which is a feature of the programmes for new players at any good club.

Rugby union is quite a complicated game, and beginners can be put off by the number of rules and regulations. Various authorities have recognised this, and several versions of rugby have been produced which are designed to introduce young players to all the skills of the game in a progressive way. These games allow children to get pleasure and satisfaction from rugby, without becoming frustrated by it.

There are two main competitive team versions: *New Image rugby* and *mini-rugby*. Both of these emphasise skills, activity and enjoyment.

New Image rugby

This is a new development which is rapidly growing in popularity. It is a fast running and passing game in which boys, girls and adults can all take part at once. New Image is "touch" rugby, in which the ball must be passed as soon as the player with the ball is touched in the correct manner. Any number of players is permitted, and the size of the pitch and the length of the game can be altered to suit the age and ability of the players. The teams are split up into forwards and backs, but as the game has a high running and passing content, there should be more backs than forwards. In fact, there should be no more than five forwards, regardless of the overall number of players in a team. Also, because there is no pushing in the scrums, the forwards do not have to be the biggest players.

The rules follow those of full-scale rugby as far as possible, but there are also many important differences.

Open play

Only tries can be scored (4 points).

Players are not brought down when tackled: instead, the tackler must touch the player with the ball with two hands simultaneously, one hand on each side of the hips. The tackled player must then pass the ball *immediately* to a team-mate (no forward passes are allowed), otherwise a penalty is given.

The only kicking which is permitted is:

- to start the game
- to re-start after a try has been scored
- tap-penalties (see page 19)

Line-out

In New Image, the line-out is much more of a practice routine than a fierce contest for possession. Two lines of forwards face towards the touchline as usual, and another throws the ball to them. It must be caught *above head-height* by a member of the team throwing in, who must then be bound – scrum-style – by two of his team-mates. The ball is immediately dropped and back-heeled to the scrum-half for passing on to the backs. The opposing team are not permitted to move until the ball is in the hands of the scrum-half of the team throwing in.

All players other than the forwards and scrum-half must be at least ten metres from the mid-line of the line-out.

Determined 9-year-olds play mini-rugby

Scrums

The scrum forms up in the usual manner, with three in the front row and two behind. The scrum must hold firm, but no pushing is allowed, and the opposition cannot strike for the ball. The scrum-half puts in the ball, and it has to be hooked and fed out through the feet of the side whose scrum-half put it in.

As with the line-out, the backs must be at least ten metres from the mid-line of the scrum.

Size of field

There is no fixed size for a New Image field: with large teams, a full-size rugby pitch can be used, but it may be reduced to a half or less for very small teams.

Mini-rugby

Mini-rugby was introduced a number of years ago as a means of encouraging, teaching and coaching youngsters. The aim is for them to be playing full-scale rugby by the time they reach their early teens. It is a game for nine players: five backs (scrum-half, outside-half, centre, wing, full-back), and a scrum consisting of four forwards, two in the front row and the other two forming a second row. The flanker joins the scrum on the same side that the ball is put in.

The game is usually played across a standard rugby pitch, using the five-metre lines as goal-lines for teams aged ten and under, and using the touchlines as goal-lines for older players.

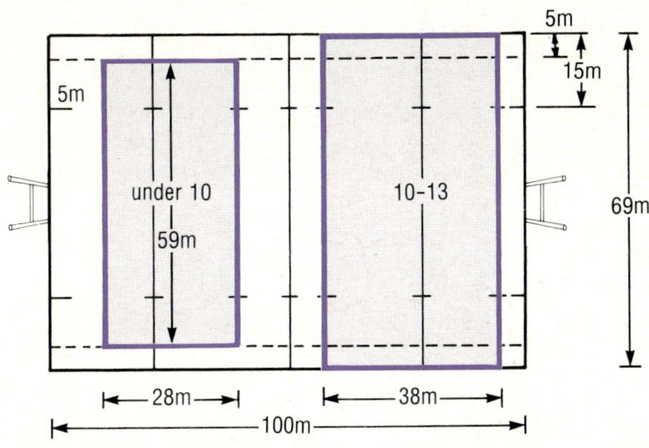

Figure 10 Suggested use of a rugby field for mini-rugby

The recommended size of the pitch and duration of play are as follows:

Age	**Size**
under 10	59 m x 28 m
10–13	69 m x 38 m

Age	**Duration of play**
7–9	2 x 15 mins
9–11	2 x 20 mins
11–13	2 x 25 mins

Play progresses as in the full-scale game, except for the following points:

- *No* fly-kicking ("an indiscriminate and uncontrolled kick at the ball") is allowed. If this happens, a scrum is awarded at the point where the ball was kicked.
- A tap-penalty is given to the opposition if a kick goes directly into touch from outside the kicker's 15-metre area.
- At all penalties the opposition must be at least 7 metres away.
- Kicking at goal is not allowed from a penalty kick.
- Teams of under-eights do not attempt to kick conversions, and under-nines and under-tens take all conversions from directly in front of the goalposts.
- The offside line for backs at a line-out is 5 metres back.
- For the under-eight age group, one coach per side is allowed onto the pitch during a game to encourage and direct his players.

Mini-rugby has introduced thousands of new players to the game. Parents can be confident that their children will gain a good and safe grounding in the game at a club with a lively mini-rugby section.

11 Getting started

If you have the good fortune to go to a school where rugby is played, you have no problem! Otherwise you should take the alternative of contacting a local rugby club.

There are many rugby union clubs which cater for junior players. They usually provide facilities, equipment, coaching, competitive fixtures and often social events for age groups of six years old and upwards. You will probably find one quite easily by asking friends at home or at school, but if you have any problems, there are several good sources of information:

- The physical education teacher at school.
- The telephone directory: look in *Yellow Pages* under "Sports Clubs and Associations".
- The local public library.
- The local Department of Recreation and Leisure. Ask them to put you in touch with the Rugby Union Development Officer. In Britain, this post is a joint initiative by the RFU and local authorities to help develop the sport.
- If all else fails, write to the RFU, whose address is given on page 64, or to your own national governing body if you live outside the UK.

Most clubs play or train on Sunday mornings, and probably also hold midweek training and coaching sessions. When contact has been made, you will find that it is much more fun if you are able to persuade some friends to go along with you.

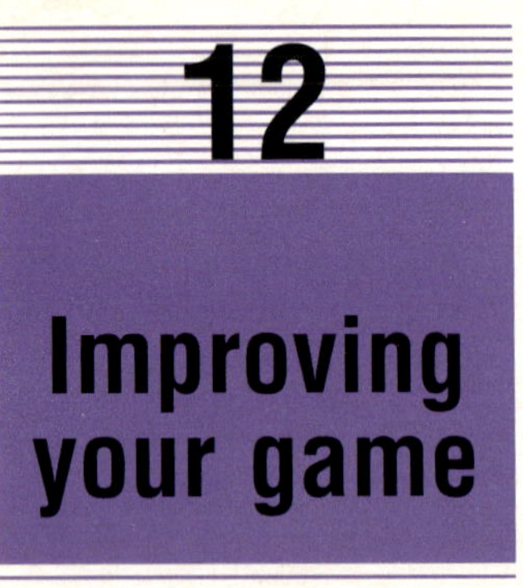

12 Improving your game

Coaching

Never miss the opportunity of instruction and guidance from a qualified coach. If you are ever in the position of having to make a choice between clubs, go for the one that offers regular coaching for your age group.

Coaching courses

In Great Britain, the RFU, in conjunction with an organisation called Rugbyclass, runs a number of courses throughout the country, usually during the summer. These courses are staffed by qualified coaches and international players, past and present. All the basic skills and strategies of the game are covered. The Rugbyclass coaching holidays are open to young players between the ages of eight and eighteen. Your club or school will have full details.

Players of fifteen and over who show potential may be invited to attend more advanced courses. These cater for players at both clubs and schools, and are organised at various levels – *district*, *county*, *division* and *national*. Players are nominated by their school or club, and invitations are sent direct to the individual.

Helping yourself

- Play in a variety of positions – do not specialise too early.
- Read about the game – not just coaching manuals and books, but also biographies or autobiographies of ex-players, coaches and other "names" in the game. Soak up knowledge from any source.
- Watch the game – live and on TV. Pay particular attention to individual players, and see how their play fits into the team's effort.

- Play other games, particularly those, such as basketball, that improve hand–eye coordination and handling skills.

Awards schemes

The RFU introduced its Proficiency Awards scheme in 1983, and it has been revised since then. There are three levels of award: *bronze*, *silver* and *gold*. The tests are supervised in clubs by the holder of a recognised coaching award, or in schools by a teacher in charge of games. The young players have to show the required standards of skill in:

1. Shuttle-run with ball
2. Catching
3. Goal-kicking (except at bronze level)
4. Scrum-half passing
5. Kicking for accuracy
6. Handling
7. Tackling

The tasks are simple, and need the minimum of equipment. Naturally, they increase in speed, distance and complexity from bronze to gold, but should all be achievable by a keen young teenager. They encourage players to learn, practise and perfect some of the many skills needed to gain maximum enjoyment from the game. *All* the required tests must be completed successfully to gain the award at each level. Cloth badges and certificates are awarded to successful candidates.

N.Z.R.F.U.
Incentive Award
for Junior Rugby Players
This is to Certify that

has achieved a satisfactory level in the following

	BRONZE	SILVER	BLACK
PASSING			
CATCHING			
KICKING			
TACKLING			
RUNNING			
SIDE-STEPPING			
SPORTSMANSHIP			

Date
Coach

Useful addresses

British Isles

Rugby Football Union
Whitton Road
Twickenham
Middlesex TW1 1DZ
England

Irish Rugby Football Union
62 Lansdowne Road
Dublin 4
Ireland

Scottish Rugby Union
Murrayfield
Edinburgh EH12 5PJ
Scotland

Welsh Rugby Union
PO Box 22
Cardiff CF1 1JL
Wales

Overseas

Australian Rugby Football Union
PO Box 333
Kingsford
New South Wales 2023
Australia

Canadian Rugby Union
1600 James Naismith Drive
Gloucester
Ontario
K1B 5N4
Canada

Fiji Rugby Union
PO Box 1234
Suva
Fiji

Fédération Française de Rugby
7 Cité d'Antin
75009 Paris
France

New Zealand Rugby Football Union
PO Box 2172
Wellington 1
New Zealand

South African Rugby Board
PO Box 99
Newlands 7725
Capetown
South Africa

USA RFU National Office
830 North Tejon
Suite 104B
Colorado Springs
Co 80903, USA

International

International Rugby Football Board
180 Whitton Road
Twickenham
Middlesex TW2 7RE
England